*So You
Don't Believe
in God?*

So You Don't Believe in God?

Russell V. DeLong, Ph.D.

BAKER BOOK HOUSE
Grand Rapids, Michigan

Copyright 1976 by
Beacon Hill Press of Kansas City

Baker Book House edition
issued September 1977
with permission of copyright owner

ISBN: 0-8010-2867-1

PHOTOLITHOPRINTED BY CUSHING - MALLOY, INC.
ANN ARBOR, MICHIGAN, UNITED STATES OF AMERICA
1977

Dedication

This book is dedicated to a man whom I greatly admire and believe in completely.

He has affected the lives of millions of human beings with his preaching, teaching, and writing.

No man in the Christian Era has touched so many and brought about changes through Christ.

Millions of our youth have had their belief in the Bible strengthened, and their faith in Christ restored by this religious statesman.

To him this volume is respectfully and affectionately dedicated:

Dr. Billy Graham

Contents

Foreword 9

Preface 11

1. Evidence, Probability, and Chance 13

2. Evidences of a Planned Universe 23
   The distance of the Earth from the sun
   The rotation of the Earth on its axis
   The Earth's orbit and the tilt of its axis
   The relationship of the moon to the Earth
   The fixed orbits of the nine planets
   The percentage of oxygen in the atmosphere
   The air pressure on man's body
   Life—its existence, mystery, and transmission
   The life cycle of oxygen and carbon dioxide
      exchange between plants and animals
   The genes and their transmission of traits
      to progeny
   The amazing circulatory system of the body
   The intricate structure of the human eye
   The mind of man

3. Creation and Evolution 52

4. If There Is No God 62

Appendix 73

Foreword

This book is remarkable for two reasons. It deals with the most important subject of life. It attempts to help those who are spiritually blind to discover God. In the second half of the twentieth century—a century which is permeated by materialism, cynicism, and hypocrisy—it is difficult to discover that there is a God who provides a meaning in life. It is not fashionable to cultivate the spiritual life because of the prevailing trend to accept or to believe only in those things which can be tested in the test tube or measured on a slide rule. Dr. DeLong tries to supplement the knowledge of the physical and social sciences with his knowledge of the spiritual life.

Albert Einstein, one of the greatest scientists of the twentieth century, would have agreed with Dr. DeLong. In his book *Ideas and Opinions*, Einstein had this to say:

> I cannot conceive of a genuine scientist without profound faith. . . . The most beautiful experience we can have is the mysterious. It is the fundamental emotion which stands at the cradle of true art and true science. Whoever does not know it and can no longer wonder, no longer marvel, is as good as dead, and his eyes are dimmed. It was the experience of mystery—even if mixed with fear—that engendered religion. A knowledge of the existence of something we cannot penetrate, our perceptions of the profoundest reason and the most radiant beauty, which only in their most primitive forms are accessible to our minds, it is this knowledge and this emotion that constitute true religiosity.

He added: "Science cannot give us a sense of the ultimate

and fundamental ends; they come into being not through demonstration but through revelation. The highest principles for our aspirations and judgments are given to us in the Jewish-Christian religious tradition." Again, to quote Einstein: "Science without religion is lame; religion without science is blind."

Reading the manuscript, I was impressed by Dr. DeLong's rigorous thinking, his immense knowledge, and his ability to convey to the reader very complex problems in a meaningful manner.

The second reason why this book is outstanding is because of the quality of its author. Dr. DeLong earned four college and university degrees from Boston University and from Harvard. He was a professor of philosophy for 27 years, a college president for 23 years, and a seminary dean for 8 years. Dr. DeLong has authored or edited 38 books and numerous articles. He knows the literature in the fields of philosophy, education, and religion. Moreover, he understands human nature and the meaning of his own life which is based on a religious foundation.

At this stage, Western civilization is largely dominated by science and technology and by totalitarian ideologies. In helping men to develop moral restraints with regard to the brutal force which governs the world and human life, Dr. DeLong shows the individual the way in which he can lead a more meaningful life. No one who reads this book will remain the same after he puts it down.

—EDWARD J. ROZEK

Professor of Political Science
  University of Colorado
Executive Director
  Aleksandr Solzhenitsyn Society

Preface

The purpose of this book is to present in nontheological and nonscientific language some logical answers to the number one question confronting man, namely, *Is there a God?* All other questions concerning the broad issues of life are meaningless if God does not exist. If there is no God, there are no higher values, no moral standards, no immortality, no accountability, no communication with the Infinite, hence no religious faith.

If there is no God, we are reduced to animals floating over the briny sea of life without purpose, without meaning, and without goals. We become merely "a hunk of flesh and a hank of hair." Nothing really matters.

But if God *does* exist, *everything* matters!

Our main premise is that an intelligent, orderly universe presupposes an intelligent Producer (Creator) and Operator. This basic idea has been a chief concern of the author for many years. When a student at Harvard University pursuing a course under the tutelage of Dr. William Ernest Hocking, Henderson's *The Fitness of the Universe* made a lasting impression. Fresh and pertinent ideas stimulated my thinking from Dr. George McCready Price's *Q.E.D.*; Dr. A. Cressy Morrison's *Seven Reasons Why Scientists Believe in God;* Dr. Leconte du Nouy's "Human Destiny: The Faith of Great Scientists" in the *American Weekly;* and Dr. Bryan Nelson's *After His Kind*.

The chief purpose of this treatise is to point out that although God's existence cannot be proven in a science laboratory, yet it is the only rational, logical hypothesis that guarantees meaning, purpose, and metaphysical values.

With millions of human beings under the dominion of some sort of Communism which denies God's existence, it is imperative that those in the free world, particularly the youth, become intellectually aware of the sound reasons for positing God as the Supreme Intelligence in this purposive and wonderful universe.

—RUSSELL V. DELONG

Russell V. DeLong, Ph.D.

Dr. DeLong was born in New England and grew up in the home of a minister. He completed his education in the East, receiving the Ph.D. degree from Boston University, and doing further graduate studies at Harvard. An internationally known evangelist, he also gave many years of his life to education, including 23 years as president of three different institutions: Northwest Nazarene College, Pasadena College, and Owosso College. He was also dean of Nazarene Theological Seminary for 8 years and was the featured speaker for 21 years on the international radio program "Showers of Blessing."

He is the author, compiler, or editor of 38 books, and has contributed to numerous periodicals. His travels of over 1 million miles have taken him to 68 countries around the world.

1

Evidence, Probability, and Chance

The key question of this book is: DOES GOD EXIST?

What are the options?

There are only two possibilities:
1. He does.
2. He does not.

It is impossible to validate any answer in the laboratory. God cannot be put under a microscope. If He *does* exist, He must be more than *matter*—He is not a *thing*. Therefore He cannot be analyzed as one would a specimen in a physics or chemistry laboratory.

If the only proof allowed is that the searcher for God must be able to touch or see or feel Him, then one ends up as an atheist, an agnostic, or a skeptic.

But there are many truths in the realm of life and

thought that cannot be proved in a science laboratory. How does one, for example, measure the love of a mother, the beauty of a sunset, the inspiration of a great symphony?

Evidence

Evidence is "ground for belief . . . that which tends to prove or disprove something." Evidence may be of two kinds: (1) direct, and (2) circumstantial.

In a criminal case, for example, direct evidence is presented by persons who witness to the crime, saying, "I saw John Doe kill Bill Brown at 4:45 p.m., April 20, 1976, as Mr. Doe left his store." The witness might be lying; he might be the victim of mistaken identity; he might have defective eyesight; he could be wrong as to the day of the month and the hour of the day. The validity of direct evidence can be assailed and destroyed.

Many times circumstances surrounding a crime and a person's involvement in it are more damning than the questionable direct testimony of persons. Hence such circumstantial evidence is more convincing than direct evidence.

A scientist cannot take God into a laboratory and prove that He exists by the use of microscopes and test tubes. But the Christian who has had a personal encounter with the Lord testifies in terms of "direct evidence." He declares, "I saw Him," "I talked to Him," "I felt Him," "I heard Him," or "I experienced Him."

Are these statements valid? Could they be the products of wishful thinking? Could these persons be mistaken? Could their declarations be figments of imagination? Could they be personalizing their ideals in a Being who does not exist any more than does Santa Claus or

Uncle Sam? This is what the skeptic and the rationalist would say they are doing.

Is there, then, circumstantial evidence that makes belief in God's metaphysical existence the most rational conclusion?

When one considers the beauties of the Earth and the glories of our vast solar system, it is quite natural that he should ask: *Where did all this beauty and order come from?* There are only three options:

1. It all came from *nothing*.
2. It all came from nonintelligent, inert, inanimate *matter*.
3. It all came from *intelligence*.

So let's consider which of these three—nothing, matter, or intelligence—is the most rational answer in the light of the known facts. In other words, what is the best option? Using the simple process of elimination which the Law of Probability follows, we shall see as we proceed, the mounting evidence on the side of option No. 3.

To illustrate this process of reasoning, consider the hypothetical case study of the loss of Sir John Cedric Bull's automobile. A comparative newcomer to the United States, he had his car stolen; and being a person of some notoriety, he was able to take his case to the upper echelons of the FBI.

The first question he was asked was: "What evidence do you have that the car was stolen? Did you see anyone drive it away?"

"No, it was just not in my parking place when I went to use it."

"Well, then," was the reply, "since we have no direct

evidence, we will have to try to find the car and work from that. I am sure you realize that with 118 million motor vehicles registered in the United States, we will need some more positive identification. In the first place, what makes was your car?"

"Chevrolet," answered Sir John.

"Well," responded the chief, "that at least eliminates all of the millions of Chryslers, Fords, and American Motors productions. We won't need to examine Gremlins, Hornets, Ambassadors, Valiants, Furies, Imperials, Plymouths, Dodges, Mavericks, Pintos, Mustangs, Thunderbirds, Mercuries, Comets, and Lincolns. And, among General Motor productions, we can pass up all Pontiacs, Oldsmobiles, Buicks, and Cadillacs. We need only to concentrate on Chevrolets. Thus, we can eliminate the examination of over 88 million other cars now operating."

"How many Chevrolets are still on the road?" asked Sir John.

"Oh, about 30 million," answered the chief. "That's not as bad as 118 million." He then inquired, "What was the year of your Chevrolet?"

"1973," responded Sir John.

"Well, that eliminates all other years before and since."

"How many 1973 Chevrolets are still running?" asked Sir John.

"Probably about 1 million," answered the chief. "What was the *model* of your car?"

"A four-door sedan."

"Well, that eliminates all the two-door models, sports cars, and trucks."

"How many four-door, 1973 Chevrolet sedans are now operating?" asked Sir John.

"Maybe 300,000," replied the chief. "What was the *color* of your Chevrolet?"

"Maroon."

"Well, that cuts it down to only about 30,000 on the road."

"Oh, yes, chief," added Sir John, "my car had a white top and a maroon body."

"In that case probably there would be only 5,000 such two-color, maroon and white, 1973 four-door sedans yet running."

"Well, one of the 5,000 would be mine," declared Sir John.

"Were there any other unique, distinguishing features of your car?" inquired the chief.

"Yes," responded Sir John. "The back window was badly cracked.

"Of the 5,000 maroon-white, 1973 four-door sedan Chevrolets still functioning, how many do you think would have a *cracked back window?*" asked Sir John.

"Probably not more than 1 percent—50," replied the chief.

"Also, my *right front fender was deeply dented,*" added Sir John. "Of the 50 with cracked back windows, how many would also have dented front fenders?"

"Not more than perhaps 5 or 10," answered the chief.

"Also, my car had a small statue of a lion on the hood; the left rear wheel cover was gone; the right rear door handle was bent; the radio was out of order; the horn was not sounding; my initials JCB were painted on the left front door; a Firestone spare tire was in the trunk; a scorched spot was on the right side of the hood; and at the bottom left corner of the windshield was a small stone chip," added Sir John.

"Well," said the chief, "we certainly now do not have 118 million vehicles to inspect in order to find your car, Sir John."

Just then an investigator rushed in and exclaimed, "Chief, I have just impounded a car—it is a 1973 Chevrolet sedan, maroon body, white top; the back window is cracked; the right front fender is dented; there's a small statue of a lion on the hood; the right rear door handle is bent; the radio is out of order; the horn won't sound; the initials JCB are on the front left door; a Firestone tire is in the trunk; a scorched white spot is on the maroon hood; and at the bottom left of the the windshield is a small stone chip.

"It must be mine," declared Sir John.

"Yes," said the chief, "all of the *circumstances* indicate that the car is yours."

So, the question is: Was the car Sir John's?

There was no *direct evidence*. There were no personal witnesses who saw the thief steal the car.

Yet the odds that there could be another car duplicating all the peculiar characteristics of Sir John's Chevrolet are a million to one against it.

A further consideration of the Sir John Bull car theft is this: Even if the thief himself should appear and say, "Chief, this is the car," this would not increase the validity of the *circumstantial evidence*.

And if the thief said, "This is *not* the right car," such testimony would not outweigh the *circumstantial evidence*. He would more than likely be accused of lying.

The circumstantial evidence with its many characteristics would not be superseded by even such direct testimony.

So, when anyone says, "There is no God" (an atheist), or who says, "I do not know whether God exists or not" (an agnostic); or who states, "I doubt that there is a God" (a skeptic); such testimony is not adequate to refute the unmistakable and innumerable incidents of purpose demanding a Supreme Intelligence as the Creator, Sustainer, and Director of this great, purposeful universe.

Probability

Dr. B. P. Dotsenko, formerly a professor and head of the nuclear laboratory of the Kiev State University in the U.S.S.R., and at present teaching at Waterloo Lutheran University, Waterloo, Ontario, Canada, makes this statement:

> The basic method of learning and understanding is trial and error. Data are results of active and passive tests, experimentations in practical life, and initial observations. . . . Verification of data is important for checking abstract conclusions (*Christianity Today;* Jan. 5, 1973).

In other words, although a theory cannot be proved as *certain,* it is accepted as *probable* because the available data make it more probable than improbable.

Probable has been defined as "likely to occur or prove true . . . having more evidence for than against or evidence which inclines the mind to belief."

When absolute proof is not, at the moment, possible, scientists construct a series of hypotheses. One of these is pursued; and if it does not correspond with the known facts, it is discarded in favor of another and then another until one is found that is nearest to or more completely conforms to their projection.

When a hypothesis is used that seems to meet most

of the requirements, then the Law of Probability is adopted until such time as a complete verification can be obtained.

Chance

Now, on the other side of the picture let us examine the improbabilities of chance as an explanation for our ordered universe. To illustrate: Suppose I have 10 pennies, each numbered 1 through 10.

I place them in my right pants pocket. What is the chance that I can pull out the penny numbered No. 1 on the first try?

Mathematically it is 1 out of 10.

Suppose I want to pull out No. 1 and then follow it with No. 2. What are the chances?

Answer—1 out of 100.

How about pulling out Nos. 1, 2, and 3 in order? 1 out of 1,000.

Nos. 1, 2, 3, 4—1 out of 10,000.
Nos. 1, 2, 3, 4, 5—1 out of 100,000.
Nos. 1, 2, 3, 4, 5, 6—1 out of 1,000,000.
Nos. 1, 2, 3, 4, 5, 6, 7—1 out of 10,000,000.
Nos. 1, 2, 3, 4, 5, 6, 7, 8—1 out of 100,000,000.
Nos. 1, 2, 3, 4, 5, 6, 7, 8, 9—1 out of 1,000,000,000.
Nos. 1, 2, 3, 4, 5, 6, 7, 8, 9, 10—1 out of 10,000,000,000.

There is only 1 chance in 10 billion that you could pull all 10 pennies in numerical sequence by pure, non-intelligent luck or by blind chance.

Now let's use a different procedure with the pennies.

Suppose I put penny No. 1 in my left pants pocket and No. 2 in my right pants pocket, No. 3 in my left coat pocket, No. 4 in my right coat pocket, No. 5 in my left

shirt pocket, No. 6 in my right shirt pocket, and Nos. 7, 8, 9, and 10 in the four drawers on the right side of my desk.

What are the chances that I can pull out No. 1 or No. 2 or No. 3 or No. 4 or No. 5 or No. 6 (or the rest) correctly? One hundred percent. There is no happenstance here—no luck—no chance. Why? Because I intelligently put them in places where I could purposely bring out whichever number I chose.

Intelligence triumphs over chance.

Consider another illustration. Suppose you had 100 marbles—99 black and 1 white. You place them all in a bottle. Now you want to reach in and without looking pull out the white one. What are the chances?

Well, again mathematically there is 1 chance in 100 that you can pull out the 1 white ball in a bottle with 99 black ones. To do it twice in a row, the chances are 1 out of 10,000. Three white balls in a row, 1 out of 1 million. Four in a row—1 out of 100 million.

On it would go, reaching astronomical odds in a short while. In fact, the odds against pulling out the white ball 10 times in a row would be 1 to 100 quintillion (100,000,000,000,000,000,000)!

Such are the odds when it comes to blind chance. Is it logical to hold that our vast, yet intricate, universe, came together by chance? The simple, mathematical odds against such happening are just too high.

Our next step will be to consider some basic facts concerning our universe—its design, precision, and balance—to which these principles of evidence, probability, and chance can be applied. Each will confront us with the question: *Could these evidences of purpose just have happened, or are they the result of intelligence?*

2

Evidences of a Planned Universe

Of all the evidences which support a belief in a Supreme Intelligence as Mastermind of our universe, none is more convincing than the delicate balance which exists between the various parts of that universe, and the infinite detail in all parts of the physical world.

Let's take a look at a few of these significant facts which support a belief in specific creation and continued superintendence by a Supreme Being.

● FACT 1:

The distance of the Earth from the sun

A high school boy asked his father, "Dad, how far is it to the sun?"

The father replied, "It is 93 million miles."

The son then asked, "Is that from the upstairs window or the downstairs?"

On such tremendous distances a few feet like that makes little difference.

But the distance between Earth and sun is very significant. If the sun were just 10% closer (about 83 million miles away instead of 93 million), we would all be burned up. And if it were 10% farther away (about 102 million miles), we would all be frozen to death. In either case human life would be impossible.

How does it come that the sun is just the right distance from the Earth to make human life possible? Did it just happen to be the right distance?

Our sun is our source of life, heat, and energy. Scientists have estimated that the heat of the sun, in its interior, is 35,000,000° Fahrenheit; while on its surface, it is approximately 12,000° Fahrenheit. What a furnace!

The sun gives off radiation of both light and heat. Astronomers calculate that it is 400,000 times as bright as the full moon (which is actually only reflecting the light from the sun) and gives the Earth 6 million times as much light as do all the stars put together. This tremendous light is the product of terrific heat.

The correct amount of heat must come from the sun to provide the temperature on Earth needed to provide a "fit environment" in which man and other life can exist. If our sun were twice as hot (24,000° instead of 12,000°), we would burn up; and if it were only half as hot (6,000° instead of 12,000°), we would freeze up.

The fact is that the distance of the Earth from the sun allows just the correct amount of heat to fall on our planet to sustain life. The amount of heat produced by the sun and the amount which reaches the Earth are in perfect balance.

Related to this is the question whether life as we know it could exist on other planets. On the basis of temperature alone, even the planets of Venus and Mars (whose orbits are nearest to that of the Earth) would be impossible places to live on. Venus, being closer to the sun, is too hot; and Mars, farther away, too frigid. Our space probes would confirm these facts.

One reputable scientist, Dr. A. Cresley Morrison, says, "It is now generally agreed that there never has been, and can never be, life in any form on any planet except the earth."

Did it just happen that man and his habitat are so perfectly matched? The odds are vastly in favor of intelligence over chance.

● FACT 2:

The rotation of the Earth on its axis

The Earth has a diameter of approximately 8,000 miles, and its full circumference is approximately 25,000 miles.

The Earth makes one complete rotation on its axis in 24 hours. On the average, a given point on the earth is facing the sun (day) for 12 hours, and for 12 hours it is in darkness (night). This means that at the equator the Earth revolves at a speed of approximately 1,000 miles per hour.

But if the Earth revolved at half its present rate (500 miles per hour instead of 1,000) it would take 48 hours for the Earth to make one complete revolution. Daylight would average 24 hours. The heat buildup in that length of time would be intolerable, particularly in the summer.

Similarly the cold during the 24-hour night would become intense, particularly in the winter. (This is actually the case in the polar regions in the winter.)

Note also that man could not sustain work for a 16-hour day, nor sleep a comparable number of hours per night. He is constituted for a 24-hour cycle.

On the other hand, if the Earth revolved at twice the speed—2,000 miles per hour instead of 1,000—it would take only 12 hours to make one complete rotation, thus making both daylight and nighttime too brief.

How does it come that the speed of the revolving Earth is just right for the existence of life, providing sufficient daylight but not too much, and sufficient night but not too much, for crop growth and human preservation? Is this balance the result of mere happenstance? Again there is the evidence of purposive planning.

● FACT 3:

The Earth's orbit and the tilt of its axis

Our Earth not only rotates on its axis 1,000 miles an hour, but also it revolves around the sun at a speed of 18 miles per second or 67,000 miles per hour.

Since, as we have noted, the Earth is approximately 93 million miles from the sun, a complete circle would total nearly 600 million miles.

Since the Earth's axis is tipped at a $23°$ angle, and always leans the same way, the sun shines more directly on the northern hemisphere during one part of its orbit and on the southern hemisphere on its other part. This is what gives us our seasons. When the sun is shining

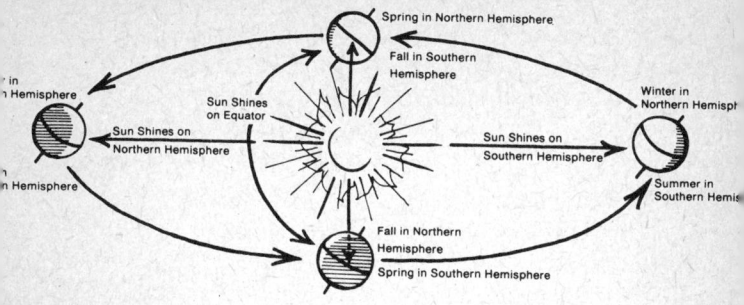

more directly on us, it is summer. At the same time it is winter in the other hemisphere.

If the axis of the Earth were upright, not only would our various seasons not be possible, but the planet would be vastly different! Scientists claim that without the tilt, the North and the South poles would be in eternal twilight. Furthermore, the water vapor from the oceans would move north and south, piling up continents of ice toward the poles and leaving a vast desert around the equator. It is also asserted that this would lower the level of the oceans, revealing large new land areas, and diminishing the rainfall in all parts of the world. Even a slight change in the tilt of the axis would create catastrophic results.

But back to the matter of the speed of the Earth around the sun. Suppose our Earth travelled at only 9 miles per second instead of 18. Such reduced speed would cause the Earth to take about 730 days to make one complete encircling of our sun. The result would be to double the length of the seasons.

This would mean that the summer would be so long the prolonged heat buildup would burn up vegetation upon which life depends. At the same time, in the prolonged winter everything would freeze up. In other words, arctic conditions would take over in the temperate zones where most of the world's people live and where most of the food is grown. At the same time the heat in the Torrid Zone would mount to intolerable levels.

On the other hand, what would happen if the Earth travelled twice as fast—36 miles per second instead of 18? The seasons would be cut in half and would not be long enough for the production of the necessary amount of food. The vast amount of food needed cannot be produced under controlled (hothouse) conditions! Man is dependent on the natural seasons.

So, how does it come that 18 miles per second is just the right speed to give us the right time needed to grow food and to prevent intolerable cold in a long winter? Here is just another example of the *"fitness of the environment."* The speed of the earth's orbit is just right to form a livable environment for man, and the tilt of the axis gives us seasonal relief from heat and cold. Did this "just happen"? Is it explained satisfactorily by chance? Would blind, inert, nonintelligent matter act this way?

The only rational conclusion is that the sun and the Earth were created, positioned, and are now maintained by a Supreme Intelligence to make this a fit environment for man.

● FACT 4:

The relationship of the moon to the Earth

I was born and reared on the Eastern Seaboard. Swimming and fishing were favorite sports. To be suc-

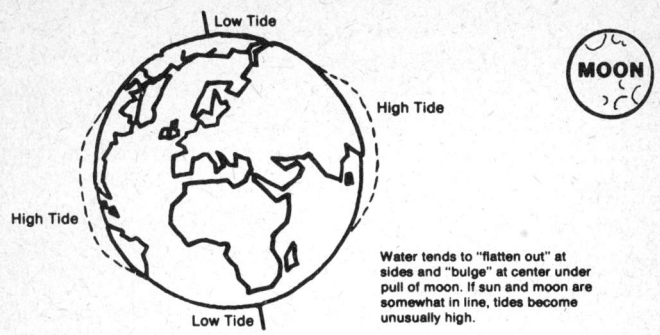

Water tends to "flatten out" at sides and "bulge" at center under pull of moon. If sun and moon are somewhat in line, tides become unusually high.

cessful in fishing and to find the most pleasure in swimming, it was necessary to check on the tides, both high and low, which occur twice each 24 hours. Not only sports but the shipping business is governed by the tides, too.

What are tides and why do they occur? Two definitions will be helpful:

1. The tide is "the periodic rise and fall of the waters of the ocean and its inlets, produced by the attraction of the moon and sun and occurring about every 12 hours."

2. "The tides are caused mainly by the moon because of its proximity to the Earth. The ratio of tide-raising power of the moon to that of the sun is 11 to 5."

The moon orbits the Earth every 28 days at an average distance of 238,857 miles. It has a diameter of 2,160 miles—about ¼ that of the Earth and a mass about 1/6 that of the Earth.

All heavenly bodies exert an attraction upon the others. The sun's pull on the Earth keeps it in orbit so it won't fly off into space. The Earth's pull on the moon keeps it in orbit too. But the moon in turn pulls on the Earth (as does the sun). They can't budge the land mass much (though they do), but they can affect the vast waters—hence the tides. These vary according to the positions of the sun and moon, but they are completely predictable. It can be determined exactly how high the water will be at any given point at a given moment.

The height of tides also depends somewhat on the topography of an area. For instance, the average tide in Mobile, Ala., is 1'6"; Baltimore, Md., 1'1"; Galveston, Tex., 1'4"; Colon, Panama, 1'1"; while in Vancouver, B.C., it is 10'4"; Portland, Me., 9'; Boston, Mass., 9'6"; and Eastport, Me., 18'2". These tides serve a beneficial purpose, in clearing debris from shores, which far outweighs any inconvenience in having to adjust to the varying water level.

Though the tides rise and fall twice a day, hundreds of millions of people around the world are safe and unharmed. Why? Because the distance of the moon from the Earth with its gravitational pull is so exact that it creates a predictable environment for man.

But if the moon were 40,000 miles nearer (200,000 instead of 240,000 miles), there would be 35- to 50-foot tides twice a day, inundating a large part of the Earth's land. Human existence would be possible only on the hills and mountains. Millions of food-producing acres would be lost.

So how does it come that the size of the moon, its distance from the Earth, with its gravitational pull, are just right for the existence of man on the Earth? Did it just happen that way? Or did nonintelligent matter make these purposive arrangements on its own?

Only a purposeful planning by a Supreme Intelligence who positioned the moon, the sun, and the Earth and who worked out the relationships of size and distance could create such a condition.

● FACT 5:

The fixed orbits of the nine planets

Here we have perhaps the greatest argument supporting the concept of purpose in the universe, particularly as related to the Earth as a unique heavenly body.

It is most interesting to study the chart concerning the sizes of the planets, their distances from the sun, and the length of time it takes them to circle the sun. Mercury (3,000 miles in diameter) is the smallest; and Jupiter (88,600 miles), the largest. Mercury is also nearest

---

The Solar System

Sun—864,000 miles in diameter
  Rotates once every 26 days

Planet	Diameter	Distance from Sun	Orbital Time
1. *MERCURY*	3,000 miles	36,000,000	88 days
2. *VENUS*	7,700 miles	67,000,000	225 days
3. *EARTH* (1)	7,900 miles	93,000,000	365.26 days
4. *MARS* (2)	4,230 miles	142,000,000	686.9 days
5. *JUPITER* (12)	88,600 miles	483,000,000	11.86 years
6. *SATURN* (9)	72,000 miles	886,000,000	29.5 years
7. *URANUS* (5)	30,880 miles	1,783,000,000	84.02 years
8. *NEPTUNE* (2)	39,930 miles	2,794,000,000	164.8 years
9. *PLUTO*	25,000 miles	3,670,000,000	248.42 years

Numbers in parentheses indicate the number of moons (satellites) each planet has (if any).

The earth's moon is 2,165 miles in diameter and circles the earth in 28 days at an average distance from the earth of 238,857 miles.

to the sun (36 million miles), while Pluto is the most distant (3.67 billion miles). As to orbiting time, Mercury circles the sun in only 88 days, while Pluto takes 248.42 Earth years. Note also how huge the outer planets are in comparison with the four inner ones.

The speed of the various planets in orbit is quite different. For instance, Mercury travels at the rate of 30 miles per second, Venus at about 3½, Jupiter at about 6, Mars at 15, and our Earth about 18. Distant Pluto swings along at about 10,000 miles an hour and still takes about 250 Earth years to make one trip around the sun.

The speed of the planets is matched to their mass to hold each one in a specific orbital path around the sun. So certain and unchanging is that orbit that scientists can predict exactly where any one planet will be at any given time. We can shoot a rocket to Mars by aiming at the spot where Mars will be when the rocket arrives months later. Furthermore, our scientists can tell to the second when that meeting will take place.

How can such predictions be made? Because heavenly bodies are controlled by physical laws. They are orderly and always follow exact paths and keep to precise times. And remember, what is true of our solar system is true also of the vast universe of which we are only a tiny part.

Truth is possible only under two necessary circumstances—(1) that an orderly mind within is functioning, and (2) that an orderly universe without is operating. If these conditions prevail, a rational man can declare something true about an orderly universe.

With a disordered mind and/or a chaotic universe, nothing could be known.

How does it come that a universe with its billions of

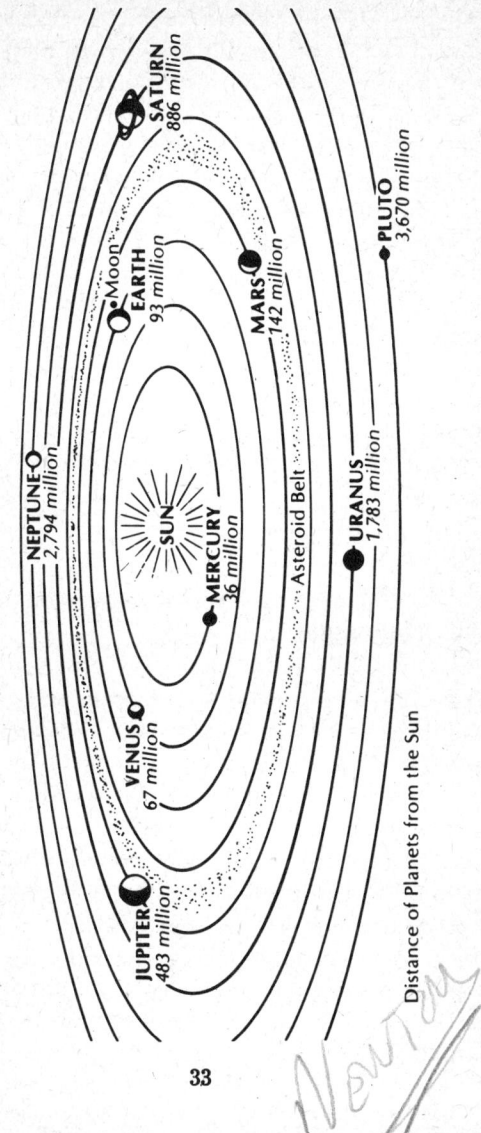

Distance of Planets from the Sun

heavenly bodies, can function without collision, friction, or tragedy? Could such order result from mere chance? Could it all have "just happened" to come out this way?

The fourteenth psalm begins by declaring, "The fool hath said in his heart, There is no God." David must have thought this to be a very important truth, because he repeated the same assertion in opening the fifty-third psalm. It is not a facetious statement. It is profoundly true. Only an illogical, irrational mind could attribute all of the wonders of the universe to chance, inert matter, or non-intelligence.

Reason demands the assertion that only a Supreme Being is powerful enough and wise enough to have produced such a vast order. And only an all-powerful One could maintain it and cause it to function with precision and purpose.

● FACT 6:

The percentage of oxygen in the atmosphere

The three vital functions of human and animal organisms are: *respiration, circulation,* and *digestion.* These regulate life—if any fails, death is inevitable.

Oxygen is the most important element in the respiration and circulation process. In respiration, oxygen from the air is transferred to the bloodstream, which in turn carries this life-giving substance to the body cells.

The atmosphere is a gaseous envelope surrounding the Earth. The main part (the troposphere) next to the Earth extends approximately 50,000 feet upward (about 6-10 miles). Beyond this are the stratosphere and other layers where the air becomes increasingly thin. These extend as far as 600 miles from the Earth.

We are concerned only with the layer in which we live and move (and fly). This blanket is composed of gases and some water vapor and suspended pollutants. The principal gases are nitrogen and oxygen; but there are minute quantities of argon, carbon dioxide, hydrogen, neon, helium, krypton, and xenon. The respective percentages of these are: nitrogen, 78%; oxygen, 21%; the remainder, 1%.

Man (and animals) *must* inhale oxygen or life ceases. It is in respiration that the oxygen is transferred to the bloodstream which in turn carries it to the cells for building and rebuilding purposes. If there is not sufficient oxygen in the air one breathes, he soon dies. Airplanes flying above 6,000 feet pressurize the cabins, one of the reasons being to keep an adequate oxygen supply. Man's system is adapted to the oxygen available at his level.

Now, if the percentage of oxygen in the air were only 10% instead of 21%, man and beast could not live. On the other hand, if the percentage of oxygen were doubled, there would be a highly flammable situation, for oxygen feeds fires. Every time an electrical storm occurred, the lightning would ignite the surrounding landscape. It would be virtually impossible to put out a fire, and so existence would be impossible. Readers will recall the death of three of our astronauts—Virgil I. Grissom, Edward H. White, and Robert B. Chaffee—while testing an Apollo spacecraft. A spark ignited the highly oxygen-charged cabin and not only burned the astronauts to death, but also probably smothered them by using up all the oxygen in the flash fire. If our air contained 50%

oxygen, ignition would occur and destroy not only the environment but all human beings.

So we ask ourselves, how does it come that the correct percentage of oxygen (21%) is just the right amount to guarantee life and also is the safe percentage to protect from fire? Man's atmospheric environment is just right, not because of some chance arrangement of gases. It must be the result of a Supreme Intelligence who "put the pieces together."

The only rational, logical deduction is that the atmosphere is the result of a Supreme Being who constructed a fit environment for the crowning product of His creative genius.

● FACT 7:

The air pressure on man's body

As was noted earlier, the Earth is surrounded by a blanket of atmosphere. This envelope is divided into several layers—troposphere, stratosphere, mesophere, thermosphere, ionosphere, and exosphere—extending approximately 600 miles above the Earth's surface.

At the Earth's surface, the air is very dense but rapidly thins out as the altitude rises. The pressure it exerts at sea level is about 14.7 pounds per square inch. In other words our human bodies have 14.7 lbs. of weight exerted on every square inch on our legs, arms, torso, face, head, feet, etc. But our bodies are built to withstand this pressure, so we are not aware of it.

However, if the pressure were increased to 25 lbs. instead of 14.7 lbs., we would be crushed. Or, conversely, if the air pressure were only 5 lbs., instead of 14.7, we would in effect explode. This is why men working in deep mines where the pressure is very great must come to the surface gradually, and why the cabins of high-flying airplanes must be pressurized.

So we face again the same old question: Is this perfect balance of pressure the result of a happenstance or the action of nonintelligent matter? Or was it worked out by a Supreme Intelligence?

● FACT 8:

Life—its existence, mystery, and transmission

Life baffles all of us, scientists included. Where did it come from? How did it get here? By what means is it sustained?

The study of genetics is the scientific specialization dealing with origins. The basic root of the word is the same as that of the word *genesis* (an origin, a creation, or a beginning).

For many years it has been predicted that geneticists would solve the mystery and come up with a formula for producing life. So far the prophecy has not been actualized, and many thinkers discount the possibility that it ever will.

We simply assert that life comes only from God and cannot be duplicated or produced by chemical combinations or the fusion of various elements.

We can land men on the moon and return them with phenomenal accuracy, yet we cannot create life.

By our inventive genius we can construct automobiles, transport pictures through the air in full color, build "almost human" computers, surround ourselves with gadgets of all kinds, yet we cannot produce life.

We have all the elements necessary. We can simulate

the temperatures needed; we can provide either a solid, liquid, or gas base; yet we have not been intelligent enough to produce life itself. We can supply the needed number of quarts of blood, hair, bone, tissues, arteries, kidneys, liver, heart, brain, and lungs. In other words, we can furnish all the essential parts of the body—even hook them all together—but we cannot put *life* into them.

It appears that here we have reached the limits of man's creative ability. TV—yes; space missions—yes; computers—yes. But life—no! If it is possible, why with all of our know-how and scientific expertise have we not found the secret?

Someone has put it this way: Life is a *musician,* teaching birds to sing, frogs to croak, lions to roar, and the human to break forth in triumphant song.

Life is an *engineer*. It designs torsos; coordinates muscles, levers, and joints; causes the tireless beating of the heart and the marvelous circulation of the blood. It designs dandelions, shapes flowers, and impels insects to carry pollen.

Life is a *chemist,* giving taste to our fruits, pungency to our spices, and perfume to our roses.

Life is a *protector* and *provider*. It gives its creatures food, legs for movement, protective armament, horns, jaws, and claws, It provides ears for sound, eyes for sight, noses for odors, and wings for flight.

What life is, no man has fathomed. It has no weight or dimension. Its force will crack a rock, or build a mighty tree and hold it upright against gravity and storms for a thousand years.

From whence has life come?

There are only four possible answers:

1. From *nothing*. This is nonsense (no-sense) to have *every* thing come from *no* thing.

2. From *nonintelligent matter,* that is, from atoms, electrons, neutrons, infinitesimal particles; or from pure, physical energy. This option tends to be unscientific because it makes a greater come from a lesser.

3. From *blind chance*. This is irrational. It begs the question. It attempts to answer with what we are asking. What is chance? Where does it get its power and its purpose?

4. *Intelligence*. This is the only option that meets the demands of the norms of a rational mind. Only a Supreme Intelligence can explain life and sustain it.

● FACT 9:

The life cycle of oxygen and carbon dioxide exchange between plants and animals

Respiration, commonly referred to simply as breathing, is the act of *inhaling* and *exhaling* air. To be more technical, biologists define it as "the sum total of the physical and chemical processes in an organism by which oxygen and carbohydrates are assimilated into the system and the oxidation products, carbon dioxide and water, are given off."

As has been indicated earlier, oxygen is the most necessary gas for human life. It is colorless and odorless and constitutes 21% of the atmosphere.

Carbon dioxide is also a colorless, odorless, incombustible gas present in the atmosphere. It is a product of respiration in which man (and animal) breathes in (inhales) oxygen and breathes out (exhales) carbon dioxide.

The blood carries the inhaled oxygen to the cells of the body and brings back the waste products (carbon dioxide) to the lungs for exhaling.

At the same time, the "vegetable world" (such as plants, shrubs, trees, vegetables, and flowers) exude (give off) oxygen and breathe in carbon dioxide. In this respect, the animal and vegetable worlds are complementary. So vital is this relationship that one would die without the other.

Man's body is so consituted that he must have oxygen, while vegetables (in the broad sense) are so constituted that they must have carbon dioxdie.

How does it come that the earthly environment is so constituted as to meet this mutual need—oxygen for man and carbon dioxide for plants? D:d this fortunate arrangement "just happen"?

Does it make sense to endow nonintelligent matter with such purposeful planning? The most rational option is that it was all prearranged and planned by a Supreme Intelligence.

● FACT 10:

The genes with their transmission of traits to progeny

In every cell nucleus, male and female, animal and man, are found genes. A gene is defined as "the unit of heredity transmitted in the chromosome that, particularly through interaction with other genes, controls the development of hereditary character."

The genes are the controlling factor as to what every human being shall be. They are the ultimate keys to all human, animal, and vegetable characteristics.

The genes determine whether a child shall look like his father or mother; be blonde, brunette, or redhead; be tall or short; have a long or a pug nose; have blue, gray, or brown eyes; have a low IQ or a high one.

The genes determine the species. They lock the door so that there can be no crossing of species. A cat is always a cat; a dog, a dog; and an elephant, an elephant. No oak tree ever bore chestnuts or wheat seed produced corn. The boundaries are fixed and immutable by the genes. They hold the ancestral record and determine the species and design.

Illustrations could be multiplied as to how colts, puppies, and kittens—yes, children—resemble their parents. What determines the similarity and fashions the offspring? The genes.

Yet the genes are infinitely tiny.

Morrison declares that if all the genes in the world could be gathered up, they are so infinitesimally small that a thimble would hold them all.

Incredible it is that in a small bit of protoplasm—stuff—tinier than a pinpoint—too small for the human eye to perceive and almost too small for the most powerful microscope to detect—is the gene. And that set of genes has wrapped up in its tiny self my ancestral record, the characteristics of my progenitors, the peculiarities of my species, and the idiosyncrasies of my special line of foreparents. This little speck—a gene—gets into a newborn human body and fashions my daughter or son to look like me and to reproduce my peculiar physical characteristics.

No wonder the Psalmist cried out: "I will praise thee; for I am fearfully and wonderfully made" (Ps. 139:14).

So the question: Can these infinitesimal bits of protoplasm containing all the ancestral traits and characteristics, be explained satisfactorily other than by accepting the action of a Supreme Intelligence?

● FACT 11:

The circulatory system of the body

The *Reader's Digest* carried a reprint of an article which originally appeared in *Today's Health*, entitled "Your Amazing Circulatory System." It stated that "the world's most remarkable transportation system is the circulatory system of your own body." It went on to give the reasons why:

1. It is longer than any United States railroad. It has between 60,000 and 100,000 miles of route.

2. The heart pumps the exact blood flow required by any tissue or organ, carrying food to, and wastes away from, several hundred trillion customers—the body cells.

3. The circulatory system is self-repairing. A pinprick destroys hundreds of minute capillaries. Instantly new ones sprout. If you get a minor injury, immediately a cottony web forms over the wound, trapping red cells and building a sealing clot.

4. Blood flows through the system at the rate of 5 quarts per minute—7,200 quarts every 24 hours. Arteries are more than mere tubes—they are living and pulsating. Arteries control the flow, sending blood to the tiniest ends of the circulatory system.

5. Arterial blood transports amino acids for tissue repair, sugar for energy, minerals and vitamins, hormones and oxygen. On the return trip through the veins, the blood carries off carbon dioxide.

6. The liver is the blood's master regulatory organ, controlling the amount of amino acids which go to the muscles and storing glycogen for body needs.

7. Fats and proteins are delivered by the blood, iodine for the thyroid gland, phosphorus for the teeth, calcium for the bones.

8. A quart of oxygen is in circulation all the time. Hemoglobin, the iron-containing protein, which gives the blood its red color, is the carrier of this life-sustaining gas. Hemoglobin gives up oxygen and takes aboard carbon dioxide.

9. There is an amazing network of capillaries, the microscopic junction points between arteries and veins. These capillaries are incomprehensively small—1/3,000ths of an inch in diameter.

10. The kidneys are elaborate filtering devices containing 64 miles of piping. Every 24 hours these small, bean-shaped organs handle 180 quarts of filtrate from the blood, eliminating impurities.

11. The blood in the adult body contains 30 trillion minute red cells. They are born and destroyed at the rate of 72 million a minute. Their life-span is 30 days. One of the jobs of the liver is to screen out aged red cells and at the same time salvage their vital iron. The blood also contains white cells. These engulf and eat invading bacteria thus preventing disease.

12. The circulation system is amazingly durable. Even the heart rests between beats. Most of the time no more than 10% of the circulatory system is working to maximum capacity.

The complex task of blood traffic-control is handled by the vasomotor center at the base of the brain. When one is resting or sleeping, the system all but shuts down. When the person becomes active, the system springs into action. Muscles will need added glucose, and carbon dioxide must be carried away.

After meals one needs more blood for digestion. Swimming after meals, therefore, can be dangerous, for there isn't enough blood for both the digestive organs and the muscles. The vascular motor center goes into action, sending blood to the digestive organs first. Muscles, being momentarily starved, are likely to cramp.

Such a complex building and rebuilding system as circulation is certainly did not come together by haphazard chance.

How could millions, yea, trillions, of particles be assembled into a meaningful, purposeful function by the mere chance relationship of these cells? Again we must posit a Master Designer.

● FACT 12:

The intricate structure of the human eye

Both the human eye and the ear are "fearfully and wonderfully made," but the eye is particularly amazing. A more complicated and at the same time more efficient mechanism is hard to imagine. So let's take a look at the eye—retina, lens, optic nerve, rods, cones, cornea, iris, pupil, muscles, sclera, and so forth.

In simple terms, the eye is like a camera. Light passes from the object through the lens and is focused on the retina at the back of the eye. But notice that the

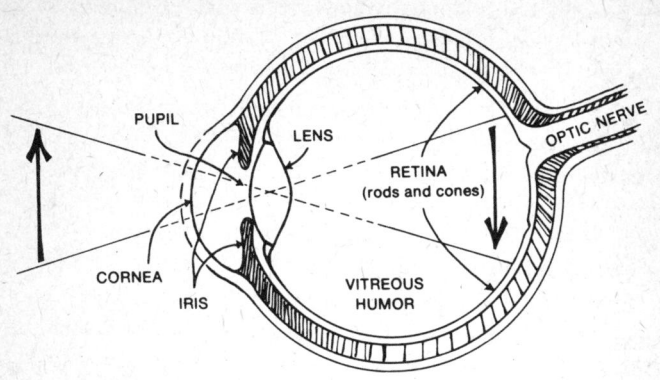

thickness of the lens is automatically controlled so that the image is always sharp. At the same time the iris opens up or closes according to the amount of light. (In dim light it opens wide; in bright light it closes down, else the retina would be damaged.)

The retina itself is made up of nine layers, yet is no thicker than a piece of paper. The innermost layer is made up of 30 million rods and 3 million cones, all connected by nerve fibres to the brain. The cones are what allow us to distinguish colors.

These are arranged in perfect relation to each other so what the eye gathers can be interpreted by the brain. Furthermore, as with any lens, the image focuses on the retina upside down. The brain automatically makes the adjustment so we don't live in a topsy-turvy world.

Another marvel of the eye is that the octave of perception is raised from light to heat, making the eye sensitive to color. We can see a colored picture of the world with all its multitude of hues. (Can you imagine a world of only blacks, whites, and grays—like all photographs used to be? What beauty would be lost!)

Accentuating the miracle of sight is the fact that all of the unbelievable adjustments of lens, rods, cones, nerves, and all else, must occur simultaneously. Each part of the eye must work with the others, or sight is impossible. How could one necessary factor know and adjust itself to the requirements of the others?

Note also the perfect coordination between the two eyes. Though they see the same object, there is a slight difference in the viewpoint—about three inches apart. This makes it possible to judge distances. That is, we see things in relationship to each other—one object is near, others farther away. And all this is done automatically! All of the parts of each eye—lens, cornea, iris, pupil, retina, muscles, nerve fibres, etc., work together—and when they do—bang!—*eyesight*.

Can the miracle of the eye be satisfactorily explained by blind chance? Could all this intricate machinery be put together without a design and a Designer? The only rational conclusion is that there is a Supreme Intelligence back of it all.

● FACT 13:

The mind of man

We come now to the most important and the highest evidence of purpose in the universe—the *intelligence of man*.

Dr. A. Cressy Morrison opens his discussion of "The Mind of Man" with this statement:

> How strange it is that in the innumerable varieties of animal life, living and extinct, there is but little evidence of mentality other than instinct until we come to man himself. No animal has left a record of its ability to square a stone or to count ten or understand the meaning of ten.

The instincts of animals are awe-inspiring and defy the efforts of science to explain them. Ants, bees, fish, mammals, birds all act beneficially and at times, apparently, purposefully. Dr. Price describes the marvelous activities of the wasp who catches a grasshopper, digs a hole in the ground, stings the grasshopper in just the right place to anesthetize it so that it lives on in the form of preserved meat. The children of the wasp eat without killing the insect on which they feed. The wasp must have done all things right the first time, or there would have been no further wasps.

Instinct causes purposeful actions. How can this be explained except that these instincts are designed for preservation and procreation?

Without depreciating the wonders of instinctive actions, it must be observed that "instinctive" action is not "intelligent" action caused by thought and produced by a deliberative selection of an act among several possible alternatives.

For instance, a dog does not say to himself, "What should I do now? Gnaw on that bone, chase that rabbit, run downtown, or lie down in the shade of that tree and rest?" What he does is determined by the strongest instinct of his physical organism at the moment—whether it be hunger, pugnacity, excitement, or rest. He operates on instinct alone—he does not think, or ponder, or choose.

In all of the universe, whether we speak of planets, satellites, continents, mountains, nations, cities, buildings, trees, animals, chairs, tables, automobiles, television sets, airplanes, computers, or any other thing—none possesses a mind; none is intelligent.

Man alone has reasoning power. He can think—no animal can think, nor can any inanimate thing.

Man can remember great, inspiring, *past* events; he can also *imagine* and anticipate *future* probabilities and possibilities. And he can *choose* desired, possible ends.

Man has the incredible *ability to create*. He can build the pyramids, conquer the oceans, construct a Taj Mahal, tunnel through mountains, erect bridges, patrol the skies, harness rivers, produce electronic apparatus, split the atom, invent the computers, discover new elements, and create musical, literary, and artistic masterpieces.

The mind of man has invented machines and intricate mechanisms to outdistance the speediest antelope, outfly the fastest bird, see farther than the eye of an eagle, and hear sounds unperceived by the most wily beast. Man has exceeded animals in all categories.

Man has developed speech and language so that only man can communicate verbally with each other.

Man has a conscience which impels or restrains his actions. He knows right from wrong. He lives on an ethical plane and acquires moral values. Such is not true of animals or things.

Man is the only living entity that has the sovereign power of choice. He is autonomous—self-directing. He can choose right or wrong, the high or the low, good or evil, the better or the best. Man is free. Liberty is his greatest posession.

In short, man is a person possessing an intellect, emotions, and a will. He has what we call *personality* or personhood. In the opinion of the author, the most important word in the vocabulary of man is *personality*, including both divine as well as human personality.

Once again we are confronted with the question: Is the intellect of man to be explained by nonintelligence? If one assumes this position, he violates one of science's accepted presuppositions, namely, that a lesser cannot produce a greater. To say that the intelligent mind of man must have been created by nonintelligent matter is not only illogical but unscientific as well.

The only option by which to explain human intelligence is by a Supreme, suprarational Intelligence. A *Supreme Being* is the only possible and probable explanation of a *human being*.

In Summary

Let us now look at these 13 factors together in order to get a blanket perspective. Then let us honestly ask: Can this array of indisputable facts be cast aside as merely a happenstance of unorganized, unplanned forces of nature? Did this "fit environment" (to use again Henderson's phrase) for man's arrival and survival come about by a capricious, unpurposed combination of fortunate fusions of chemicals, temperatures, and spacings?

FACT No. 1—The favorable distance of the sun from the Earth, producing the correct amount of radiation so that we neither burn up nor freeze up.

FACT No. 2—The rotation of the Earth on its axis, the speed of which provides a favorable daily cycle for man's existence.

FACT No. 3—The Earth's 365-day orbit of the sun, combined with the precise tilt of the axis, which produces the necessary seasonal cycle needed for the growing of food.

FACT No. 4—The pull of the moon upon the Earth, which produces the beneficial tides but avoids devastating inundation.

FACT No. 5—The fixed orbits of the nine planets, which indicate precision and order in the universe and prevent catastrophic collision.

FACT No. 6—The precise percentage of oxygen in the atmosphere, which sustains life but protects us from uncontrollable combustion.

FACT No. 7—The correct air pressure on man's body, which allows normal activity upon the Earth's surface and for a limited distance above and below.

FACT No. 8—The very existence of life itself and the mystery of its transmission, which science can neither fathom nor duplicate.

FACT No. 9—The life cycle of oxygen and carbon dioxide exchange between plants and animals, which enables each to survive.

FACT No. 10—The infinitesimal genes which control the unique, hereditary characteristics of each organism.

FACT No. 11—The incredible circulatory system of the human body whose 60 miles of tubes carry the needed building and repair substances to every part of the body.

FACT No. 12—The intricate structure of the human eye, which is typical of the fact that the entire human body is an amazing mechanism.

FACT No. 13—The uniqueness of man's intelligence, which sets him apart as a creature of reason, choice, and responsibility.

Think again of the 10 numbered coins. The odds on being able to pull from one's pocket each coin in numerical sequence from No. 1 through No. 10 are 1 in 10 billion. On the other hand, we noted that if each coin were placed purposely in specific locations, each could be pulled out in correct order because of intelligent planning.

There is not one chance in trillions that the 13 facts or evidences of purpose we have cited could have "just happened." Granted, one or two might have come about by accident (though this is hard to conceive), just as it would be possible to pull coin No. 1 out of one's pocket by chance. But to pull all 10 coins out in numerical sequence, or to explain all 13 facts on the basis of chance is beyond reason.

The only rational conclusion is that these facts exist because of the creative and controlling hand of a *Supreme Intelligence*.

3

Creation and Evolution

No study of the Source of all things would be complete without a consideration of the various theories of evolution versus biblical creation. The problem is more than a biological issue; it has to do with the very fundamentals of faith and reason—one's concept of God.

Down through the centuries there has been an unfortunate conflict between *faith* and *reason* and between *science* and *religion*. Actually, there should be no battle at all. If they do differ, either the *faith* is unfounded or the *reason* illogical, or both are in error. Within the realm of scientific knowledge and religious truth, there should be no contradictions.

Science is concerned primarily with *processes*—how things work. It is not concerned with *origins* or *causes*. This is as it should be, for *science* is interested only in *facts*—things as they are. *Values* and the interpretation of *facts* is the field of *philosophy* and *religion*. Science specializes on the "how"—philosophy on the "what" and the "why."

Whenever a philosopher poses as a scientist, he leaves his field as an expert and becomes an amateur in a strange land. On the other hand, when a scientist steps into the field of philosophy, he is no longer an authority either.

Scientists search for facts verified and validated by experimentation. Let them continue their glorious explorations and continue their magnificent discoveries.

But when a scientist declares that there is no God—no ultimate Cause—and that there are no values higher than the physical and natural, he surrenders his credentials as a scientist and becomes an amateur philosopher.

Such is the nature of the controversy between creation and evolution. It is not the purpose here to present the "pros" and "cons" of each or endeavor to resolve the difficulties. We intend merely to state the position held by each and make a few pertinent observations.

The battle is really between Biblical Creation and Naturalistic Evolution. However, to better understand the total picture, various types of evolution theory need definition.

I. Biblical Creation

Those philosophers and theologians who affirm Creation accept the biblical account as recorded in the first book of the Bible, the Book of Genesis. Here is how it reads—

In the beginning God created the heaven and the earth (v. 1).	Here is the *origin* of all things: "*In the beginning God . . .*"

And the earth was without form, and void; and darkness was upon the face of the deep (v. 2a).	This is the description of the original chaos of unorganized matter.
And the Spirit of God moved upon the face of the waters (v. 2b).	Here is the dynamic—the power, the *cause*—"*The Spirit of God.*"
And God said, Let there be light (v. 3).	The origin of *light*
And God made two great lights; the greater light to rule the day, and the lesser light to rule the night: he made the stars also (v. 16).	The appearance of *sun, moon,* and *stars*
And God called the dry land Earth; . . . the waters called he Seas (v. 10).	The establishment of *continents* and *oceans*
And God said, Let the waters bring forth abundantly the moving creature that hath life (v. 20).	The appearance of *fish* and *animal* life
And God created . . . every living creature . . . after his kind (v. 21).	"*After his kind*"—after his species. This phrase appears 10 times in the creative record.
And God said, Let us make man in our own image, after our likeness (c. 26).	The arrival of *man.*

So God created man in his own image, in the image of God created he him; male and female created he them (v. 27).

The crowning capstone of God's creative genius is man.

Briefly, this is the story of creation. (For more details read the entire record in chapters 1 and 2 of the Book of Genesis.)

It will be noticed that the Sacred Record is in perfect accord with scientific knowledge—the natural order of procedure from chaos to man. All the parts which make up our world come together: the *heavens, sun, moon, stars, space, time, matter, force, mineral, vegetable, animal, man, intelligence, morals, spiritual life*. And all are ultimately related to God.

In the *beginning*—GOD.
In the *process*—GOD.
In the *ending*—GOD.

II. Evolution

A. *Naturalistic Evolution*

In a nutshell, Naturalistic Evolution holds that all that now exists came from some preceding and lower condition. This process extends back millions of years to some hazy and cloudy beginning. All is explained by natural development without the need for a Supreme Being. It deals only with processes; not *origins*. In brief, proponents frankly state, "We don't know how it started or where it all came from; but here it is now, and this is how it seems to have come about and how it functions today."

There have been many readjustments and restatements of evolution since the days of Darwin, Lamarck, De Vries, Mendel, and others.

Some have made a real effort to build a bridge between creation and evolution. A brief discussion of some of these ideas will illustrate how men have grappled with the problem, striving to retain the claims of *naturalistic evolution* and the truths of *biblical creation*.

B. *Theistic evolution*

This is an attempt to accept "evolutionary processes" but to inject God into the picture as the First Cause in order to explain origins and to make His power the dynamic which makes the "evolutionary processes" function.

For the theistic evolutionist, each "gap" in the evolutionary march forward (and hopefully upward) is filled and explained by God's intervention. Thus, theistic evolution is a sort of fusion of the truths of creation and the hypotheses propounded by naturalistic evolution.

C. *Bergson's Creative Evolution*

This theory attributes the "push up" in the process through (1), the *inanimate-mechanical stage* to (2), the *animate-organic stage* to (3), the *human life-intelligent stage*, to the "Elan Vital" or life principle. Bergson allows for the introduction of novelty but attributes its cause to this "life principle." There is a constant battle between the "cosmic urge" upward and the "cosmic drag" downward. Some critics of Bergson claim that his theory is one which permits invention (introduction of the new) and process but does not make place for values.

D. *Matthews' Psycho-Tropic Evolution*

This theory posits a "purposive spirit"—a sort of "world-ground" pushing up from the inanimate, to animate life, to human life, to intelligence, to immortality and spirit. He contrasts the biological and psychological progression with many very interesting and fascinating comparisons. Matthews goes from strife between individuals and their environments to the "survival of the fittest" in the biological, to the "arrival of the fittest" in the psychological; to behavior versus self-psychology; to skepticism versus idealism; to adjustment patterns versus the aspiration of persons; to Nirvana versus the Kingdom. In his system he will acclaim a "psychological basis," a philosophical ultimate; a pedagogical ideal; and finally, a religious ideal. His conclusion is stated in these words—"The goal of Evolution—can it be anything else than Immortality?"

E. *Morgan's Emergent Evolution*

Professor Lloyd Morgan's theory of Emergent Evolution received very favorable acclaim when first proposed in his book *Emergent Evolution*.

The theory appears to incorporate the main principles of biological evolution but in addition posits *intelligence*, with God as the Causative Force in the evolutionary process. Morgan illustrates his theory as follows:

Mind	
Life	INTELLIGENCE
Crystals	ORGANIC
Molecules	MECHANIC
Atoms	

G O D

All novelty in the process emerges in each successive stage upward. However, these new elements seem to subsist in each lower form potentially and not injected from without.

Morgan's final statement in his book affirms his attempts to put God in the evolutionary process:

> We acknowledge God as above and beyond. But —unless we also intuitively enjoy His Activity within us, feeling that we are in a measure one with Him in Substance, we can have no immediate knowledge of Causality or of God as the Source of our existence and emergent evolution.

Rather than seek to analyze these theories, our purpose here is to make *one important point*.

In all four of these modified evolutionary theories we have considered—Theistic Evolution, Bergson's Creative Evolution, Matthews' Psycho-Tropic Evolution, and Morgan's Emergent Evolution—all are agreed that Naturalistic Evolution is not sufficient; it does not solve the problem. Something must be added—the *"Elan Vital"* of Bergson; the *"purposive Spirit"* of Matthews; or *"God"* of Theistic Evolution.

If one accepts *any* evolutionary theory, it is still pertinent to raise these points:

1. What about the *origin* of matter, space, things, and power?

2. The apparent "gaps" in any evolutionary hypothesis must be explained either by having an *outside power* insert something into the process or by having an *inside power* interject novel items into the process.

In order to make this point more lucid, let us briefly select and describe one evolutionary theory called "The Nebular Hypothesis." This was formulated by Laplace in the nineteenth century. It is the theory that the solar system evolved from a mass of nebular matter.

Possibly 5 million years ago (maybe 10 or only 3), there was a large cloud or ball of "fire mist"—nebular matter. After some time this mass began to revolve—and with increasing rapidity—generating great heat. Suddenly a hunk of this ball shot off from the main core —and then another—and another, etc.—and formed the *planets*. From some of these hunks there were lesser shoots which became *satellites*. Eventually these hunks cooled off and stopped "shooting."

In planet Earth, land masses were formed and water filled the depressions between. After many eons a *one-cell animal* appeared in the water; later, a *two-cell;* and then *multicellular* living organisms developed. They eventually moved onto dry land, developed means of locomotion there (legs and wings), and developed other adaptations to the environment. Finally, through many stages the higher and larger animals arrived; and then then *multicellular* living organisms developed. They eventually moved onto dry land, developed means of locomotion there (legs and wings), and developed other adaptations to the environment. Finally, through many stages the higher and larger animals arrived; and then came the came the apes and finally modern *man*.

"Intelligence" appeared in man, making possible great inventions, sublime literature, and beautiful art, lifting man to moral and spiritual heights above the other creatures. With this elevation came religion and the aspiration for the higher values and finally, in some instances, to the claim of immortality.

It should be pointed out that the Nebular Hypothesis and any other of the evolutionary theories leave more unanswered questions than their advocates level against the proponents of creation.

1. Where did the "fire mist" come from?
2. Where was it? In space? If so, where did space come from? Or what is space?
3. What started the "fire mist" in motion?
4. How do you explain the intense heat?
5. What caused the planets finally to revolve in separate, definite orbits? And what caused the satellites to "shoot off"? (By the way—some of the satellites revolve in the opposite or reverse direction of parent planets. What turned them around?)
6. Where did the *life* in the one-cell animal come from?
7. How did this develop into a two-cell and later into a multicellular organism?
8. When did man arrive?
9. When did "intelligence" appear, and where did it come from?
10. Where did man get his ideas of moral values, of God and immortality?

As indicated earlier in the discussion, these questions are outside the field of Science. The answers must come from elsewhere. They are the province of the theologian and the philosopher.

Every human being is somewhat of a philosopher. Be he scientist, educator, artist, industrialist, or farmer, doesn't he ask the great questions:

Who am I?
Where did I come from?
What is life all about?
Why am I here?
Whither am I bound?

If scientists would refuse to negate religion; if evolutionists would abstain from ridiculing creationists; if philosophers would stop considering science as an enemy —yes, even if creationists would cease their attacks on evolutionists, all could more openly and harmoniously search for the truths of creation (science) and the truths about the Creator (religion).

A scientist is a *man* before he is a scientific expert. A philosopher is a *human being* before he is the personification of wisdom.

Man needs facts but also faith. He needs knowledge but also wisdom. He needs science but also philosophy. He needs the friendship of man but also the fellowship of God.

Science tells us the "whats" of life. Philosophy reveals the "whys" of living.

Science and technology teach us "how" to make a *living*. Religion and philosophy tells us how to make a *life*.

Science tells us how to reach out and master things. Philosophy inspires us to reach up and *let God master us*.

4
If There Is No God

There is nothing that has a greater effect on man, morals, meaning of life, purpose, mission, commitment, righteousness, compassion, mercy, kindness, and concern than the *belief in God*. If God does not exist, invaluable imperatives for good and happy living are seriously damaged or fatally obliterated.

Let us explore the field under four alliterative headings (the four *Ms*).

1. *Man*
2. *Meaning*
3. *Morals*
4. *Mission*

1. Man

If there is no God, man is not an *immortal soul*. He is not a creation of God as described in the *Bible* (Gen.

2:7): "And the Lord God formed man of the dust of the ground, and breathed into his nostrils the breath of life; and man became a living soul."

Man's *body* came from the "dust of the ground," but his *soul* came from the breath of God.

So man is a duality—*body* and *soul*. He has a *material* nature and also a spiritual nature.

If there is no God, man has no soul, is not a spirit, and does not have an immaterial essence. He is merely a creature, the result of naturalistic, evolutionary processes. He is only the highest of natural things.

If there is no God, all of man's activity must center around the needs or desires of the physical body—for that's all there is to be concerned about.

If there is no God, man is reduced to bones, skin, blood, and tissue.

If there is no God, man's body at death disintegrates into dust—that's his end.

Of course, *if there is no God*, man is not immortal—there is nothing to live beyond the grave. Any consideration of eschatological events is a waste of time, for there is no activity for man beyond the grave. Death becomes a great big period—a blank wall, a dead end, a futureless destiny. Life is all over.

2. Meaning

One of the greatest difficulties faced by our youth today is that during the past 25 years, we have taken from them the *raison d'etre*—the "reason for being."

They have been taught that they are super-evolved animals; that there are no immutable moral standards; that belief in the soul is passe; and that God is merely a myth created by superstitious old fogies.

So the philosophical "highest good" becomes whatever will bring pleasure and satisfaction to the *body*. Conversely, whatever brings pain and distress to the body is *evil*. Therefore if nicotine, alcohol, dope, or sex bring pleasure, that is all the *truth* and *good* one needs.

Actor Jack Lemmon, appearing on the "Today" show on television, made the comment, "People have nothing worthwhile to live for—there is no meaning in their lives." So it is for millions—it is just tomorrow—and tomorrow—and tomorrow—and finally, death (and increasingly by suicide).

We must find some way to put *meaning* back into the minds and hearts and lives of human beings.

Some time ago, *This Week* magazine carried the following article under the heading "We Want Meaning in Our Lives":

> What most people want—young and old—is not merely *security,* or *comfort* or *luxury,* although they are glad enough to have these. Most of all, THEY WANT MEANING IN THEIR LIVES.
>
> If our era and our culture and our leaders do not, or cannot offer great meanings, great objectives, great convictions, then people will settle for shallow and trivial substitutes.
>
> People who live aimlessly, who are satisfied by shoddy experiences, have simply not been stirred by alternative meanings—religious meanings, ethical values, ideas of social and civil responsibility or high standards of self-fulfillment.
>
> This is a deficiency for which we all bear a responsibility.... *This is the challenge of our times.*

The Bible asserts that "the fear of the Lord is the beginning of knowledge: but fools despise wisdom and instruction" (Prov. 1:7). The word "fear" here connotes the wrong meaning for most minds. Too many interpret the verse as if we must stand in constant fear of the power of God to punish or destroy us. The meaning here is, rather, "reverential awe, especially toward God."

The wise man is calling upon us to stand *reverently* in awe at the majesty, power, greatness, goodness, wisdom, and righteousness of the Creator, Sustainer, and Architect of our great universe. When one loses this sense of reverence for God, he becomes blase, possibly blasphemous, and soon loses reverence for father and mother, home, school, church, law, morals, and spiritual values.

Job, one of the greatest and wealthiest men in history, from his unparalleled experience declares, "Behold, the fear of the Lord, that is wisdom; and to depart from evil is understanding" (28:28). The Psalmist twice asserted, "The fool hath said in his heart, There is no God" (Ps. 14:1; 53:1).

If we would preserve our moral structure, give impetus to higher living, provide inspiration for happy lives, and give our youth a *raison d'etre,* we must put God back in our thinking, in our homes, in our schools, in our businesses, and most important, *in our lives.*

Dr. D. Elton Trueblood, a great philosopher, says, "Men cannot live well either in poverty or abundance unless they can see some meaning and purpose in life, which alone can be thrilling" (*Alternative to Futility,* p. 15).

3. Morals

We have reached new highs in education, industry, medicine, and invention, but have fallen to new lows in crime—murders, thefts, rapes, suicides, and sex perversion.

What has happened?

The basis for morals has been abolished. God has

been relegated to the cemetery for unwanted concepts.

The fundamental question is—*can there be a dynamic ethics that is not rooted and grounded in metaphysics?*

Why should anyone be *honest?*
Why should anyone be *truthful?*
Why should anyone be *moral?*

Without a *belief in God* there is no imperative for one to *do right.*

If there is no God, and if I am not a soul, the only guide for one's acts is the social mores of the times—what the majority of society vote to be right. Tomorrow their action may be changed. Today's prohibitions may be tomorrow's approbations.

Why should one do right, tell the truth, or be honest? Only to avoid legal sanctions—jail, fine, or other punishment. If I can commit evil acts, be dishonest or untruthful, and *never be found out*—it is OK. The motto of such citizens is—"Nothing's wrong except getting caught. So be cute, careful, prudent, and smart. There is no God and there are no immutable standards. The Ten Commandments are Hebrew myths. Eat, drink, and be merry, for tomorrow we die."

Immanuel Kant, one of the greatest philosophers of all time, declares, "All morality rests upon three postulates—God, freedom, and immortality." In other words, there are three shoulders or foundation stones upon which all morality must stand:

1. Belief in God.
2. Belief in life after death—immortality.
3. Belief that man is free to choose right or wrong.

Without these basic principles, morality is built upon the shifting sands of atheistic relativism.

Dr. Hans Driesch, one of the great modern German philosophers, in his book *Ethical Studies,* asserts, "It is only upon a Metaphysical foundation that Ethical studies become more than a game in Aesthetics." He further states, "For every day and unsophisticated life, metaphysics is the theoretical and religion the practical foundation of everything. . . . It is a fact that for those who absolutely deny immortality, all things are at bottom ethically indifferent. Such men as a rule will be atheists and materialists."

Another great authority in the field of psychology, Dr. William McDougall, makes this prediction: "I believe that if science should continue to repudiate the belief in any form of life after death, morality will continue rapidly to decline among all civilized peoples, and will, before many generations, have passed away."

His prophecy is certainly beginning to come true today.

4. Mission

If there is no God, there is no powerful imperative to impel one to achieve something worthwhile. Life has no objective—there is no goal, no purposive end.

Belief in God provides high ideals, worthy goals, worthwhile objectives. It makes life rich and achievement thrilling.

In New York City, an 18-year-old girl took a revolver and blew out her brains. She left a note behind saying, "I've had every thrill a human being can have, and life isn't worth living." On a physical basis her statement was probably true. She had never caught a glimpse of the high plateaus of moral and spiritual goals inspired by a belief in God.

A group of motion picture stars were on a TV panel

show. In the course of the discussion one said, "I have never known a Hollywood star that is truly happy." Others on the panel did not dispute the statement.

Happiness cannot be found in the muck, mire, and sewers of physical debauchery. *Things* have no power to bring inner peace. They may bring external, transient pleasure but not permanent, internal happiness. When purpose in life goes out the front door, perversion comes in the back door.

Life must have *meaning, purpose,* and *mission.*

More than 90% of all the great materpieces of literature, art, and music have been produced by men who believed in and revered God. It is also true that the great majority of outstanding leaders in business, statesmanship, education, and the professions have been profound believers in God.

Thousands of statements from such preeminent leaders could be cited. As samples of a few, consider the following (italics mine):

DR. ROBERT A. MILLIKIN—*Nobel Prize winner and pioneer in cosmic rays*

> The two great pillars upon which all human well-being and human progress rest are: (1) the spirit of *religion,* and (2) the spirit of *science,* or knowledge.
> But—the supreme personal and individual opportunity of everyone, without exception, is with respect to the *first* (religion).

DR. ALBERT EINSTEIN—*Nobel Laureate; theory of relativity*

> It is the conviction, akin to religious feeling, of the *rationality* or *intelligibility* of the world that lies behind all scientific work of a higher order.
> This firm belief, a belief bound up with deep

feeling, in a *superior mind* that reveals itself in the world of experience, represents my conception of God.

DR. A. H. COMPTON, *Nobel Prize winner*

Faith gives the courage to live and do. Scientists, with their disciplined thinking, like others, need a basis for the good life, for aspiration, for courage to do great deeds. *They need faith to live by.*

The hope of the world lies in those who have such faith and who use the methods of Science to make their visions become real. Visions and hope and faith are not part of Science. *They are beyond* the nature that Science knows. *Of such is the religion that gives meaning to life.*

DR. P. LECOMTE DU NOUY—*Father of numerous medical and biological discoveries. Author, "Human Destiny"*

The agnostic and the atheist do not seem to be in the least disturbed by *the fact that our entire organized, living Universe becomes incomprehensible without the hypothesis of God.*

DR. KIRTLEY F. MATHER—*Longtime professor of geology at Harvard University*

We live in a Universe, not of *chance* or *caprice,* but of *Law* and *Order. Its Administration is completely rational and worthy of utmost respect.*

DR. ROGER J. WILLIAMS, *Longtime director of the Biological Institute, University of Texas*

Do I believe in God? The answer is yes. The God who really matters in human life is the God who gets into people and *gvies them noble purposes* and *ideals,* and endows them *with the spirit of love.*

DR. KARL T. COMPTON, *longtime president of the Massachusetts Institute of Technology*

A very able soldier and statesman concluded an address by saying that the desperate need of the people can be summed up in three words: (1) Food, (2) Fuel, and (3) Faith.

We may, he added, supply *food* and *fuel* through individual or national charity, but these will be only temporary and superficial unless we can somehow also provide these masses of people with a *basis for faith*.

DR. ALFRED C. LANE, *formerly vice-president, American Academy of Arts and Sciences*

Belief in God is necessary to the progress of humanity. I say that Geology does not favor the theory that there was no plan in the Universe until man arrived. There are definite signs of God's plan in the story of the earth as recorded in Geology.

DR. GUSTAF STROMBERG, *staff astronomer for 29 years at Mount Wilson observatory*

I believe that behind the physical world we see with our eyes and study in our telescopes and microscopes, and measure with our instruments of various kinds is *another, more fundamental,* realm which cannot be described in physical terms. In this *non-physical realm* lies the *ultimate origin of all things,* of *energy, matter, organization* and *life* and consciousness.

The fourth moon-team of the United States composed of *Col. David R. Scott,* 39, and *Lt. Col. James B. Irwin,* 40, roved about the moon's surface for 18 hours and 37 minutes covering about 17½ miles and gathering 226 pounds of surface material.

Jim Irwin, in addition to his report of great scientific value, also recounts his experience in sensing God's presence. As he looked back to the beautiful Earth with its scintillating colors and to the starry heavens about him, he received a new conception of God.

Colonel Irwin says,

What really touched my soul was the fact that I

could feel God's presence so strongly, and in so many different ways.

I felt God's presence on the moon more than I have ever felt it here on earth; and I came back from the Apollo 15 flight to find it had changed my life. (*Decision*, January, 1973).

The result is that he now is devoting his time addressing young people of college and high school age, emphasizing the importance of religious purpose and commitment.

Astronaut Frank Borman affirmed his belief in God when he said, "The more we learn about the wonders of our universe, the more clearly we are going to perceive the hand of God."

All of the above statements of outstanding educators, scientists, and leaders, support the thesis of this book, namely, that a *belief in God as the Supreme Intelligence is rational and of great importance.*

If there is no God—

- —We are lonely orphans in a godless universe.
- —We live like animals and die like beasts.
- —We have no *raison d'etre*—no reason for living.
- —We have *no soul,* no immortality.
- —There are *no moral values,* no sense of oughtness.
- —There is *no realm of truth.*
- —There are *no immutable standards;* "right" and "wrong" are relative.
- —There is *no Christ*—for if there is no God, He had no Son.
- —The Church is but a man-made organization, and worship a waste of time.

—Religion is, as Communists claim, a deceitful opiate.

—Nothing is either intrinsically good or evil.

The loss of these *values* and *institutions* is a colossal price to pay for atheism, agnosticism, or even skepticism.

In the light of all the evidence presented in this book, it seems rational, reasonable, practicable, and even scientific, to believe that a *Supreme Intelligence* is the best option proposed. If there is a God, all these deeper values become meaningful. They are the stuff that true life is made of.

Appendix

Philosophical Arguments for God

The present book has dealt almost exclusively with the Teleological Argument with some references to the Cosmological. Here, in a nutshell, are the basic philosophical arguments which point to belief in God.

1. The Ontological Argument
(*Ontos*—being + *Logus*—word)

The Ontological Argument is the only *a priori* argument (that is, not derived from experience—not empirical). All other arguments are *a posteriori* (from experience).

Stated in brief: We have an idea of the most perfect Being, a Being than whom a greater or more nearly perfect Being cannot be conceived. A Being that is nonexistent is not as great as one who does exist. This most perfect Being is God. Therefore—God must exist. Anselm is generally regarded as the originator of this argument. Immanuel Kant, the great German philosopher, considered the Ontogolical Argument as the greatest argument for proof of the existence of God.

Rene Descartes, the French philosopher, presented the Ontological Argument with a different slant. It runs as follows: We find that all of our ideas come either from *within* or from *without*. An idea so great as "God" cannot be found in empirical experience; therefore, it must have been divinely planted in my mind. This Being must be greater than either external matter or internal mind. Therefore—God must exist as the Implanter of this greatest of ideas.

2. The Cosmological Argument
(*Cosmos*—world + *Logos*—word)

This argument is as follows: Everything begun owes its existence to some producing cause. The universe is a thing begun and owes its existence to a Cause which is equal to its production. This Cause must be indefinitely great.

The argument requires three things:
 1. The principle of causation.
 2. The dependence of the cosmos.
 3. The inadequacy of the forces of nature.

The Unmoved Cause must be a cause of all existing, active things—hence, the need for God. He is regarded as the First Cause.

3. The Teleological Argument
(*Telos*—end + *Logos*—word)

The Teleological Argument in brief: A design infers a Designer; a purpose, a Purposer; architecture, an Architect.

In syllogistic form:
 1. Design presupposes a Designer.
 2. The world everywhere exhibits marks of design.
 3. Therefore the world owes its existence to an intelligent Author.

The Teleological Argument is a doctrine of ends, or of rational purpose, in the construction of the cosmos (world), as exemplified in the foresight and choice of ends and the use of appropriate means for their attainment.

Most of the treatment in this book supports the Teleological Argument to prove the existence of a Supreme Intelligence.

4. The Anthropological Argument
(*Anthropos*—man + *Logos*—word)

This argument in logical form is much like the Cosmological and Teleological arguments. It proceeds from the nature and endowments of mind to the proof of divine existence. Man's constituent nature demands a Higher Being whose nature exceeds and transcends man. Man, being a person, demands a Supreme Being who also is a Person. Personality is the highest we know. Therefore, God could not be less but rather far and beyond the finite personality of man—an Infinite, Absolute Person.

5. The Moral Argument

In brief, the argument is as follows:

1. Man's intellectual and moral nature must have had for its author an intellectual and moral Being.

2. Man's moral nature demands the existence of a Lawgiver and Judge.

Man's emotional and voluntary nature demands the existence of a Being who can furnish in himself a satisfying object of human affection and an end which will call forth man's highest activities and insure his highest progress.

The idea of obligation, or of oughtness, is an idea of pure reason. Consider these facts:

1. By the very constitution of our nature we have an immediate perception of right and wrong.

2. These moral perceptions are distinct from all other notions or judgments of the mind.

3. These judgments are spontaneous and self-originated.

4. This ability of the spirit, with its sense of obligation, its endorsement of right and condemnation of wrong, is called "Conscience."

5. Such a moral judgment demands the idea of a *moral law*.

6. A *moral law* involves the idea of a *Lawmaker*.

7. This *moral law*, and this *Lawmaker* outside of ourselves, involves the idea of responsibility to God.

Immanuel Kant declared, "Every man has a conscience and finds himself inspected by an inward censor —Duty! Thou great, thou exalted name! Whence thine origin?" (*Metaphysics of Ethics*, p. 245).

The only answer which reason can give to this question is *God*, the great moral Lawgiver.

8. It is this moral nature in man as revealed by conscience that furnishes unanswerable proof of the moral character of God.

> If I must be *good*—must not also the universe be *good*?
>
> If I must be *righteous*—must not also the universe be *righteous*?
>
> If I must be *truthful*—must not the Supreme Being be *truthful*?
>
> If I must be *honest*—must not the universe also be *honest*?
>
> If I must be *moral*—must not God be *moral*?

As a final argument let us consider what is perhaps the strongest argument for God from a philosophical standpoint.

6. The Dialectic of Desire

The word *dialectic* means the logical progression of thought in investigating the truth of any theory or opinion. It considers a thesis, an antithesis, and proceeds to a new synthesis.

The following presentation I owe to Dr. Edgar Sheffield Brightman, longtime Borden Parker Bowne Professor of Philosophy at Boston University. This material, taken from his lecture notes, was later incorporated in his book, *A Philosophy of Religion* (Chap. 8, sec. 7).

Step No. 1: Desire for Pleasure (enjoying)

Desire must be for something.

a. There are qualitative differences in pleasure.

b. Some pleasures are to be preferred to others: hence, pleasures must be judged by some other ground of preference. Why is one better than another?

c. We desire not pleasure alone, but the objective grounds of its permanence. Hence, transition to physical things.

Step No. 2: Desire for Physical Things (having)

a. Things are desired, not for their own sakes, but for the experiences they will produce.

b. More than *things* are necessary for conscious satisfaction. Hence, they are not a coherent standard.

c. Possession of *things* is valueless without conscious *activity*. Hence, transition to activity.

Step No. 3: Desire for Activity (doing)

a. Essential element in life of value.

b. But *activity* must be for some *end*. Hence, mere activity is not a coherent value.

c. That *end* must not merely be *individual* but *social*. Hence, transition to other persons.

Step No. 4: Desire for Other Persons (sharing)

  a. Esential to a life of value—love.

  b. But persons are valued not as mere existences but as "carriers of value." Hence, it is not coherent to say that value is social.

  c. Society is a progressive realization of ideals. Without ideals it would be valueless. Hence, transition to ideals.

Step No. 5: Desire for Ideals (planning)

  a. Expresses need for intelligence, truth, reality.

  b. Pleasure, things, activity, persons, are relative to ideals.

  c. Ideals are overindividual and impersonal.

  d. Problem: Can the system of our ideals be thought of as obectively real?

  e. The antinomy of the ideal

  Thesis: An ideal must be beyond our personality.

  Antithesis: An ideal must be realized only in personality; apart from it, it is a mere abstraction.

  Synthesis: True value must be an objective union of the ideal and personality—a Supreme Person.

  Hence, transition to Supreme Person.

Step No. 6: Desire for the Supreme Person (worshipping and cooperating)

  A coherent account of the objectivity of value and its necessary relation to personality